An Everything
Joe Elliot

SPUYTEN DUYVIL
New York City

Library of Congress Control Number: 2024946196

Just what you secretly wished for: Jackie DeShannon in a field of large plastic flowers from the 1960's, sea creatures darting past the corner of Avenue M and East 17th in Brooklyn, a good looking (though possibly stale) apple . . . it's like Joe wrote a book and put all of humanity, which includes you, in it. But humanity seems different now, way more interesting—revelatory even—when looked at through the Elliot prism. You might recognize yourself in that prism, but you're no longer just you: you and humanity's malfunctioning, incoherent business are suddenly, and brilliantly, ALIVE.
    —Sharon Mesmer

Sitting down to read Joe Elliot's *An Everything*, you'll as easily be swiped off your chair and transported to "a booth at a diner" or to "El Mozote" or the "roofs of Arles" as to "disparate worlds that imply the infinite/and instantaneous passage of time." His imagery climbs on jungle gyms of juxtapositions tempting you to follow it through "the saturated color of MunchkinLand" only, like wonder, to be "made to work the assembly line" and end "bottled up and sold off," leaving you to contemplate the tacit gravity of "light spilling out" of an open fridge and the silent guffaw of a funeral parlor pop up ad. Like a post-modern Marcus Aurelius, Elliot treats readers to his bare-hearted consciousness in these meditations that vacillate wildly between brushing one's teeth and the dense silence that meets a lonely Universe…between particular identity and nothingness or a world "busy with birds /and filled with their song"… between the revolution of youth and the capitulation of old age. Indeed, throughout this volume, you can't help but suffer the author grappling with mortality, and, as "when a poet reaches the end," "you feel you finally/understand them, and maybe/ even yourself. . ."
    —Tamra Plotnick, author of In the Zero of Sky"

Joe Elliot's new book, *An Everything*, is a celebration of the ordinary and the daily. Joe's the New York poet, the teacher, father, entertaining, insulting and every so often tossing a student's hand grenade poem back out the window. I love the humor and the surprises—when the universe becomes Sister Mary Theresa. Or a bird song becomes greater than the sky. Or at night while hanging wet towels on the railing or changing a lightbulb, suddenly an awareness of the "infinite and instantaneous passage of time." These poems are funny, deep and wise, and I was very glad to read them.
    —Barbara Henning

for Ranger and Tiger,
mismatched
siblings of mischief,
long-lived
furballs of love

Entirely Peopled

Bedizened

The Unthinking Middle of Everything

Entirely People'd

At first,

the sentences seem artless,
as if the narrator

were sitting across from you
in a booth at a diner,

and her intimate and eager
talking relaxes you,

and you feel the natural
urge to respond,

tell your story,
share your burden.

But then you realize
this person across from you

isn't your older sister,
isn't your best friend

from grade school.
She is a poet,

and she's not going to give you
your turn.

She's arranged the sentences
so artfully

that there's no way in,
no opening,

so that suddenly
the check's arrived,

and her place opposite you
is already vacant,

and her western omelet
sitting on her plate

is entirely untouched
and perfect,

waiting to be photographed,
put on the menu.

for Calvin

Avoid taking a photograph with a busy background.
Remain in the right lane unless you are passing.
Keep your mouth shut. Stay within the confines of
your own skin. Why would your mind mind

the unlikely and untrustworthy ideas it produces?
To the producer the product always seems totally
presentable. To the parent each of its babies seems
totally lovable. It's a law, a kind of partisanship

that preserves the species but annihilates the earth,
which is just another word for truth. The truth
always seeks the largest context, a wider and wider
world in which you can feel more and more forlorn.

Don't ask to go home. Don't smile for the camera.
Don't crop the picture. Don't shut the shutter. Be glad
to be faceless, half-obscured by the passing
delivery truck. Pay attention to the strange letters

tagged on its flank. Be proud to be
one of the entirely un-elect.

Since they did not have a machine

I got to fill up their red kettle,
and put the kettle on the stove,
and then go take a second morning piss
(now that I am older the first one
doesn't quite do the trick). I got to get
distracted by and start leafing through
an old poetry book on the bathroom shelf
until I was summoned, when the kettle
began to whistle, back to the kitchen.

Then I got to rummage around
the cupboards and pantry for a funnel,
a large masonry jar, the paper towels,
a square section of which I tore off
and folded in quarters to make a filter,
and for the coffee itself, which I found
in the freezer and was glad had already been ground.
Then I got to scoop the coffee into the filter
which was nestled in the funnel
which was resting on the wide
mouth of the large jar.

Then I got to tip the kettle and pour
the water over the grounds with one hand,
while holding the funnel steady with the other,
and then wait while the water steeped
and slowly passed through the coffee
and trickled from the bottom of the filter
into the jar, and then I got to repeat

this process, tipping the kettle again
and again every so often when the water
level had sufficiently fallen. And in between
each of these dousings, I got to look up
out the wide window over the kitchen counter
at the wet field and the wet woods and
the wet gray sky, and see what no one else
(they were all still sleeping), just me,
was seeing at the moment, and hear
the steady drumming dripping rain.

Poem

We were walking in the park
when my son mentioned he wrote a poem
he thought was pretty funny, and went on to say
he realizes now that Late Capitalism

likes to gut the state of all its internal functions,
all its domestic programs and social regulations,
so that the only functions that are left
are external ones, the military and the police,

the means by which peoples both within and without
are exploited and made to serve. To develop
this point further he described to me
the massacre at El Mozote,

a travesty and a tragedy both promulgated and hushed up
by the Reagan Administration. For years it was as if
this crime had never happened. I was still
waiting for him to get to the funny part,

and then wasn't sure if the poem was now over
and I had somehow missed it, or if he simply
hadn't arrived at the poem yet and the realization
and illustration he'd been relating

had been serving as background material
to help me understand the poem,
which could now be understood as pure
absence, as before I could ask any follow up questions,

he abruptly terminated his speech and veered
down another path to go meet up with his friends.

Consolation

We are all dying. You are just doing
the hospital part of it, the part where tubes
and wires are stuck into your arm, your neck, your mouth.
The rule of three is also impossible

not to follow. Two's okay. Two things get together
and necessarily form a club. But the third comes along,
bringing with it difference, the possibility
of non-membership providing the basis

of choice. And when you are standing there
having to make a choice, time seems to expand,
giving your life a palpable dimension
and shape, as if it could go on forever.

Yet, this movement into the thick of things,
this always being on the brink,
is always in the context of necessity. All of a sudden
it's over, and it turns out you were just doing

the falling in love part of it, the running around
with the kids part of it, the carrying laundry
up the stairs and binding tomatoes and hopping on
your bike and riding to work part of it.

for Josie

1.

The big bullfrog on the log
is sporting a bowtie and his mouth
is parted in speech. The speech
is in the process of being received
by the smaller frogs sitting in a half-circle
on the shore. The shore is sandy,
and the sand is the period of time
you gave in to eagerness, obeyed
your childhood, if there ever was
such a thing, and the log is
that authoritarian moment when things
intruding on history show up
like a sickness you can't beat.
The bowtie is how you dress up tyranny.
The tall grasses are the walls
that make these transactions obscure,
and therefore secure. The black water
of the pond is your bottomless mind,
infinitely influenceable. O, if only
a frog were a frog and you were you!

2.

The future is the gift we keep under the tree,
never stooping to pick it up and open it.

The needles dry and fall and form a neat skirt
around the wrapped up box, lending it a gender.

Afraid it might catch fire, we carry out the dry
and brittle tree to the curb for pick up in July

finally, but the box remains. We keep putting off
opening it up, and instead kick it forward

up the street, a little further with each step,
with each day. There is nothing else to do, no

other action to take. The box waits in the corner
for the next tree to arrive in December.

3.

The bird can no longer fly.
It has been caught in the wallpaper.
Patterned, it multiplies and evolves
incrementally from white to black,
bird to fish. Now it swims in the dark
and deep school of imagination
and we want to swim there too, to
dart to and fro with others. Even for the depressive
shut in, even for the pair of ragged claws
scuttling across the floor of silent seas,
this is animate. For the ocean is not content,
but container. Whatever you are or even think you are
surrounds you, inundates you, providing you
a body to be in. You fight through
the skin's surface and take a breath.

4.

The bookmark is a pen and ink child,
black and white, laminated, exacto'd, staring out,
and the page is a forest of birches
the child would presumably wander in.

Is keeping a journal a counter-revolutionary act?
Is the personal so revolting? Should we shoot
anyone who presumes to cut and paste postcards,
who collects Rod Mckuen quotes, who is building up

an external heart? Sensitivity can take up a lot of space,
space that could be used to house the poor,
or compost the dead, or flood the market
with nothing at all. Contrivance of air. Convenience of use

value absenting itself with a quiet bow.
The chalk outline on the sidewalk is your reward
for believing in atoms. The infinite vacuum between each
the price of your having to be righteous.

5.

The photograph of the single winter tree,
leafless, standing on a bluff,
water and sky meeting on the gray
horizon, is beautiful, and gives some sense of what it might mean
to bravely go missing. The notebook itself
was also bereft. She had to glue red
endsheets to the inside covers to
make this loss her own. And thus to be stuck
there, in that bleak pose on the bluff
for the rest of her life,
which, once these parameters were fixed,
happened so quickly.

6.

Under the yellow with human
illumination awning, mostly empty
tables, but a couple of couples
lean in, talking, the white aproned waiter
standing by those you are watching.

Beyond, cobblestones catch the lemony
light that spills from the cafe,
and beyond that the shadows in which a family,
who could be dimly yours, hurries home.

Here and there windows of the dark
shoulder to shoulder houses that line the street
glow orangely. Above the awning,
and above the dark forms of the roofs of Arles, are stars
flowering, lilies floating in an enormous blue pond,

the eyes you think you recognize
lively from behind the mask,
an uncertain sparkle of gratitude
against a background that cannot be broached.

This is everything, or an everything
you once saw as everything.

7.

A frog and mouse stare at each other
from opposite ends of a very horizontal
and simple world, encountering in each other
that strangeness they do not see in themselves,
but need to to carry on without desperation
their daily rounds. The pattern is always
striving to get outside itself and unravel.
The hoodie'd cashier at the grocery store says,
'Have a good day' in a way that makes you realize
you are old and on the way out. In the dim
aisle between the stacks at the library
you encounter a child who, freshly fallen
from an old book, freezes in her tracks
and strangely calls out, presumably to her mother,
long absent, and so, in your loss that recalls
every other loss, for loss is cumulative,
and with your paw you check your arms
for fur and your face for bristly snout and teeth.

8.

Looking at the pen and ink drawing
called 'Walking with a Staff',
it takes a while to find the man
implied by the title. He is so small

and disappears into the landscape,
of which there are two. One on the top,
which is rocky and mountainous,
and the one at the bottom, the valley

with its streams and trees. The man is merely
walking in the moment, as he must,
the top of his head just touching
the weird horizon line joining these two

disparate worlds that imply the infinite
and instantaneous passage of time,
from the one he starts out in to the other one
he ends up in. This is the reason

for the staff. He needs it of course
to hold himself up.

9.

You'd rather wake up in the middle of nowhere
where the wind bends but does not break
the trees and the leaves fly headlong

from right to left just outside the helmut
shaped window. If you look even more closely
you realize there are impossible bubbles

floating by as well, weightless globes
within the globe of the world, and that world
within other worlds, and so on, all of us

weightless, floating, or might as well be,
so little can we now carry, our arms splayed out,
palms up, ready to receive the unknown

into which we are crossing. It is thus we enter
any earthen city, where daily rounds seem real and full
of things like socks and stoves and bins

of paper clips, where everything that is full
and real is timed out and planned for and pre-arranged.
But you'd rather be dis-arranged and free.

10.

Her head is lowered,
focused on her task.

On the table next to her
is a wild flower arrangement

in an earthenware vase,
and she is needlepointing

an image of this arrangement
on a cover for a pillow

on which a loved one may
lay their head. Relax. It has all been arranged.

When it's your turn
you can lay your head

in the dirt and wildflowers
will grow out of you.

11.

The strategy of distancing yourself from it
in order to grasp it more completely
was so successful you applied it to every
aspect of your life. And so, although you owned
and controlled everything, you participated
in nothing. You rolled up your windows
and turned on the AC and stereo system
to maximize your drive in the country.
You had someone else kill and butcher
the animal, someone else carry the meat
to market, a third to view and purchase it,
a fourth to prepare it, and a fifth to serve it
on a plate. And there it is in front of you,
as per your request. And how delicious
all that absenteeism is! How delusional
it is to put off the funeral, to have your sibling
cremated and put on a shelf and wait
a few months for the seasons to turn
while you plan a date that is a little more
doable for everyone to get together and
"celebrate her life!" This way, no one
has to be inconvenienced, no one has to just
stop what they're doing and drive or fly
overnight and get there for the burial
the next day. No one has to respect Death,
no one has to even participate in Death,
for mere participation is un-American
and can never win an election, for nothing
cannot be Googled and penciled in
and prepared for in a planner.

I must be 6

or 7, and am sitting
under a cool and quiet
lean-to of shadows,
and am looking up

at millions of specks
floating in the flood
of light angling
into my father's den.

The Job

The hairdresser's daughter shaved her head and moved to Portland.
The talk show host's son, just ordained a Trappist monk,
took a vow of silence. It has been several years now since the
oldest son of the insurance salesman ran away to the circus
so he could walk a tightrope, put his head in the mouth of a lion,
be shot from a cannon. The two university professors
spawned a bright and promising child who was kicked out
of middle school, high school, her first year of college,
and has been woofing her way around South America since.
The prima ballerina gave birth to a fat social worker
who wears plaid shirts and boots, who believes in data
and in the chemical foundations of creativity and mental hygiene
and in the power of the practice of clear-eyed compassion.
Both of the butcher's sons have joined the Lower East Side
chapter of the Hari Krishnas. The bus driver's teenage daughter,
having spent the summer at a farm in upstate New York,
stayed. The devout Quaker's young adult joined the Marines
on his 18th birthday. The several illegitimate children
of the thick-haired white-toothed televangelist are all living
off the grid seeking, in their own ways, to blow up America.
The bootlegger's son became a war hero, a Senator and President
of the United States. The President of the United States'
son was given a baseball franchise in Texas to manage. It is
only the child of the poet who is entirely unmanageable,
who doesn't have a chance, who earnestly attempts and fails
at a series of professions (cab driver, house painter, tutor,
food service worker, paralegal, telemarketer), only to succumb
in their early thirties to the daily writing of verse.

The Plan

Your childhood came entirely people'd.
Your many cousins and siblings and parents,
your neighborhood and school and home,
were already established. You didn't have to
do a thing. You didn't have to earn the right to
be there. You didn't even have to choose
someone to love. This was all taken care of,
and for years it seemed like it was going to go on
forever. It turned out there was a town

beyond your town. There were many more towns
and many more families in those towns
just beyond the horizon. It turned out
your parents had a childhood and a whole
period of early adulthood before you were born.
And it turned out you would have to clear out
and sell that home and move away and live
more than half of your life without this people'd
world, and this had all been taken care of.

Suffering

is a good-looking but stale apple.
You take a bite but don't like the taste.
It's not sweet enough.
It's not nearly crisp enough.
You take another bite because you want to be sure
and because you think you should keep going
because somewhere in your head you can hear
your mother saying, "Waste not, want not."
But it really is awful, and you think, "Fuck you,
Benjamin Franklin!" and stop. You put it
on the windowsill over the sink. The next week,
it has become purplish brown.
The week after, it has dried out
and shrunk and become the baleful
face of an old mother
daring you to eat her.

Power

The child digs a hole at the beach
until water starts to pool at the bottom.

He puts some shells and rocks and seaweed
in it, creating an environment.

He adds two small crabs that he's caught
and then a mussel he's broken open with a rock

and tied a string to so he can dangle it
before the crabs, enticing them into a fight,

which he will closely monitor all afternoon,
looking down at his small world of water,

which is just a few feet away
from the ocean, which is not,

nor has ever been,
open to the public.

for Maryjane

You have all the time in the world
because this is all the time there is,

and, because it can be broken down
into seconds and minutes and days and years,

it is. It breaks down and grinds to an anxious
halt just outside the kindergarten door,

right after they've taken away the wigs
and instructed us to sort and put away

the building blocks, and then opened the door
and let the beyond in. But if the world

is whole, that is to say, closed as the face
of a three year old cutting paper

or pushing a tiny shopping cart and sing-song-ing
to their plastic baby, and cannot be broken,

if beyond really is beyond
and therefore concerns us not at all,

maybe we don't have to infinitely expand
and crush everything into cinders

and fill up and pave over those spaces
that are always opening up.

You

Because you do it right away
no one else has a chance to do it.

They might do it. It's not like
they don't want to do it or are

not planning to do it. They just
haven't got around to doing it yet.

They haven't got there yet.
Their sense of timing is personal

and particular to them. So when
you go off about how you're

the only one in the office who ever
cleans the microwave, you're

really blaming others for not being you,
and who would want an office

full of you? Always cleaning,
always complaining, always

playing the martyr, always
judging others, always hogging

all the righteous service opportunities?
The office does not need an army

of you. There is only
one you. Thank you.

The Mets Need Her

When you're walking in the park
and you accidentally step on Greta's paw
because she is always underfoot,
she yelps but then goes back to what she was doing,

and when you say her name to see if she is okay,
and look at her, she looks at you
in an eager way that tells you
she hasn't taken it personally. This

isn't a grievance. I didn't even know
I was feeling grief. I had to tell someone
what I was feeling and they had to tell me
that that is grief and that that is serious.

Thus I learned that what I was feeling
was something more than what I was feeling,
that it might linger, that I might not be able to just
feel it. When Anne leaves for work,

Greta barks inconsolably at the door
for a while, which might be annoying
for the neighbors, so regular is this
outburst of feeling, but then she gives up

and gets up on the couch and falls
asleep, quickly forgetting about
her loss. This is why she would make
a terrific closer. The Mets need her.

Your hands are so good!

Look at them holding out your underpants so you can step
into them! Look at them pulling up your socks and helping you
into your shirt and shorts! Now they are tying your shoes
(and we know how hard that can be to do)! Now they are grasping
your comb and combing your hair (or what's left of it)! And now
they are gripping your toothbrush and moving it in an efficient
up and down motion, taking good care of your teeth (who are
also good, by the way)! All day long they do what you say! Soon
they will be finding your wife's feet, which will be sticking out
of the bedsheets, little rabbits poking out of their warren,
begging for attention, needing to be stroked and rubbed because
they cannot stroke and rub themselves. Someone has to provide
this therapeutic pleasure first thing in the morning, and it is
your hands who have signed up for the task. You yourself are
so preoccupied by your upcoming day that you hardly notice
these soft furry creatures waving to you from the bed and
the fleeting opportunities they represent. But your hands do.
They do it all! Soon, they will be busy at the keyboard,
completely self-effaced, obediently muting themselves into
mere extensions of your mind, (which, on its own, is captive
to your head, out of which it can never get), and it is thus
your good hands are ever getting for another, be it your head
or mind or body or some other "more important" entity,
but not so often for themselves. For who does anything for
the hands? I'm not talking about compulsory hand-washing,
something the hands themselves would rather skip,
a chore forced on them by the part of you that is deathly afraid
of any contagion they might have picked up while carrying out
all these errands for you and are now carrying home to you.
All you think about is you. You make them stand at the door,

while you hose them down and check their closely cropped hair
for bugs, before letting them in. No, it is only at night,
when you stretch out in your dead man's pose,
which your therapist has told you will help you let go of your day,
that your hands finally get some me time, palms up
towards the white ceiling, fingers relaxed, slightly curled.
And when thus you drift off, do your hands drift off too?
Do they close their eyes after all their labors?
Are they satisfied with resting themselves on your chest,
or clutching a sheet, or sliding themselves under your head
or between your knees? Do they ball themselves up into fists,
readying themselves for some battle, or go palm to palm
and pray to whatever God hands pray to? No, these are all
the human actions they take when they're on the job for us.
What configurations they take when they're off duty
and on their own we haven't a clue.

Bedizened

Novel As Foreplay

The inner lives of my characters
never want to reveal themselves to me.

They never do things that surprise me.
All I have are these puppets I have to breathe

life into constantly. But I'm not God,
and the effort to keep them going

is exhausting. I am actually right now
hyperventilating a little just thinking about it,

and the reader has begun to worry about me.
She thinks I might be crazy

to continue to push through this novel
without any real connection to the material.

She is kind. She puts her hand on
mine, stops it from flitting

over the keyboard like a moth
caught in a screened porch

in an out of season cabin. It's
getting cold. I look at her

and her quiet eyes say, "Come on. Stop
that writing. Let's go upstairs."

These Are The Ones

The danger is when you start to drift,
the unthinking ocean-liner having left
you there, to bob as you will, or worse still
it's approaching you head-on, its prow
heedlessly dividing the waves. The passengers
on the upper deck are preoccupied with
cornhole or shuffleboard or spikeball,
Uno or cribbage or strip poker. While those
on the faraway fourth deck are binge-watching
shows that elicit their regrets and fears
so that they can blame and ignore, avoid
and deny. They're on holiday after all!
Those on the third deck are reclining
in lounge chairs, taking in the sun, talking
about their neighbors, who are also reclining
in lounge chairs, taking in the sun, talking
about their neighbors, and so on, wrapping
the enormous vessel like a cumberbund
of pink frosting. The next deck down
the passengers are meeting with financial
planners, making sure their funeral and burial
expenses are in order. Those on the main deck
are out for a stroll, taking in the sea air,
and these are the ones that may spot you.

Interlude

I'm sorry. Please hold still.
What's going on? We're airlifting you

from the scene of the accident.
Accident? You know, the accident,

the mess. No it's not going to
hurt, or not that much. You were

in the middle, in the very middle
of life, and didn't know it. (Try

not to wiggle. Don't push
against the straps. We'll be there

soon enough.) But now you do. We're
almost there. Can you hear

the busses, the voices of children?
Can you see that shaft of light

coming through the window? Here
we are. *Where are we?* Hold on. I'm going to

undo your straps. Good. Now
you can get up and go back

and pick up
where you left off.

Because I was alive

I must've been breathing
fine, more or less,

without my paying too much attention,
but when they tell me

to let myself start to notice
and follow my breath, to let my mind

rest on the rising and falling
bosom of the breath, and to just breathe

naturally, I can feel that same breath
of mine grow anxious,

as if it did not know what it was doing,
as if it hadn't been doing its job

all along everyday for 61 years,
and starts to look to me for guidance

and assurance, that is when
I start to take over,

right when I should be letting go,
my uncertain mind, not resting at all,

now telling my breath when to go
in and when to go out,

now laboring
just to stay alive.

"Shit!"

A long thick brown
smear on the sidewalk.

Someone must've stepped in it
and slid,

and shouted, "Shit!"
and then tried to get it off

every few feet for the rest of the block,
each imprint a little fainter

than the last. But the dog who,
suddenly gripped by need,

had no choice but to do his
malfunctioning and incoherent

business in public; and the owner who,
unsuccessful in his attempt

to deal with their pup's
pasty muck, was ashamed,

and so abandoned the furtive job
to someone's shoe;

to the happy flies that swarm
and alight, swarm and alight;

to those microbes that mysteriously
always show up to feast;

to the rain, the life-giving
and all-forgiving rain;

and to the earth that receives
everything equally.

The Dream

The dream is in the roofline,
more specifically the cedar shingles,
the dormers and overhanging eaves.
There is something about being visibly
right under the roof, the rafters
right there, looking out an attic window
on a clear October day, that always
seals the deal, makes you reach into
your pockets for cash, gives you
something to do that is outside your
body, because inside your body
is not a place you want to go,
because you want to be a good citizen,
because you do not want to be standing
in the rain somewhere thinking about
something, you do not want to be caught
in the snow, staring across some blurry field,
your smoke signal breath drifting
and swirling in front of your eyes,
because as soon as it is habitable,
as soon as it has a roof over its head,
as soon as its head becomes your head
and its lines start to define the sky,
that is when you start to pay taxes.

Hitching A Quick

What they do not tell you
in the story of the enormous thumb

is how they had to hit that thumb
with a hammer every morning

and renew that throbbing pain,
that habitual suffering,

so that the thumb would grow in size
enough to be able to lord it over

their entire family,
that the enormity of the sore thumb

stuck out, distracting the audience
from noticing the character to whom

this enormous thumb was actually attached,
and that the thumb is there to oppose,

and is also a good thing to do to the nose
of someone, under whose thumb one

might be trying to get out from,
and, of course, extended out,

a thumb is good for hitching a quick
ride out of this town.

When

the pain of
staying shut

finally exceeds
the pain of

opening up,
the "I",

so tightly packed
unguessed at

beauty that
turns out

wasn't even
"mine",

blooms.

Into the Void

Instead of typing up and sending out
a poem about, for instance, my dead dad,
into the void, a practice that required
a certain amount of patience and fortitude

and faith, I type it into the computer
and do not have to wait, for very soon
my faceless audience begins
to emerge. Swan and Sons, a local

funeral parlor, pops up right away
in the top right corner of the screen,
as does Renewal, a dating service
for the over 60 crowd (a trim man,

salt and pepper hair, emerging from
a hot tub, frankly ogling what must be his mate).
Then the notifications start to multiply:
hair restoration products, miraculous

multivitamins, Medicare spokespeople,
assisted living communities, animal
rescue organizations, pharmaceutical
companies and their new pharmaceuticals

that promulgate freedom from all pain. It appears
that everyone is interested in my poetry!
Now I'm working on the part where
the computer both creates and performs

the poem for me, as well as generating
these aforesaid responses to it, the machine
going back and forth, back and forth,
like that, indefinitely, while I lie down

in a field somewhere whose location cannot be
revealed or sold to any interested parties.

The Dark Is Alive With Sounds

The dark is alive with sounds
is the kind of startling observation
that is startling not because of what it observes,
but because of what it implies

it didn't observe. In fact, the speaker
should be somewhat ashamed,
shivering in their tent at night
in the woods, as if they hadn't

spent the whole day in the light,
and the light hadn't been alive
too. Everything's alive. It's just
that the things we see, or

are trained to see, the landmark,
the dirt road, the winding path,
the campsite, the fire, the barbeque,
the whole world created by us,

obliviating the more than obvious
one that is not, but so insistently
is, a transcendent cacophony
we didn't notice, so busy we were

marching into the dark, driving
home the stakes, stoking the fire,
cleaning up after dinner, and staring
into the coals, to tune in.

The Mop-Top

Jackie DeShannon in a field of flowers,
the large plastic cut-out flowers
of the 1960's, when everything was a symbol
of everything else, even the rifle barrel
the guardsman was pointing at the mop-top
turtle-necked college student. Guns aren't real,
they are just a demonstration of power,
the kind you can't put your finger on,
the kind that disappears down hallways,
behind walls and glass and gates, and eventually
into landfills. That is what the bullet is for,
so you can feel it. That is what the flower is for,
so they can feel it, feel its goodness,
and so that each of them can put a little
love in their heart. Ah, the 60's! The decade
when you no longer have to think
about what people think about you,
no longer have to go to their shows
to hear some synthesized cymbals clang.

for Mr. Horowitz

I'm not that good with names.
I guess it's not going to be easy to write a poem,
even though these untagged faces
keep coming through the door,
declaring themselves home. I don't know
a single one of them. I open the fridge,
and they gravitate like a congregate
shadow towards the light spilling out.
We need that fridge to put our dead
animals in. We need to put our dead
animals in our half-alive bodies and howl.
Metabolism doesn't have a name.
Respiration doesn't have a name.
Teeth and tongue don't have names,
yet they make their homes everywhere.

The Holidays

When you see your picture
of your children at the beach
smiling into the camera,
behind which it is understood
you're standing, you're touched
exceedingly and particularly,
and, filled with this holiday
spirit, decide to affix it
to your holiday card.

When I see your picture
of your children at the beach
smiling into the camera,
behind which it is understood
you're standing, affixed to the card
you sent me, I am touched
too, somewhat and generally,
and to some extent also filled with
that holiday spirit. I mean,

I do understand that you love
and are proud of your children,
of how marvelously they've grown,
how big and beautiful they are,
there in the sun, and I do admire
this sentiment and do believe
it is appropriate, but your experience
is not my experience. Next time,
why don't you ask me for a picture

of my children at the beach
smiling into the camera,
behind which it is understood
I'm standing, and affix that picture
to your card and send that card
to me, so I can feel a little more
what you feel, and I will affix
your picture, which I already have,
to my card and send it to you.

Breath,

I like how you refuse to
let me hold on to you,

how you insist on keeping separate from me,
rhythmically accompanying me,

paralleling me wherever I go,
you on your side of the stream

and me on mine, the way a stubborn
shadow clings to the heels,

or the way the moon at night
never lets your car get away,

how you are both a welcome guest
in the cavity of my chest,

(yet the kind who knows when to leave
discreetly, warming the world

a little when they do), and also a ghost
who's always hanging around,

an animating and permeating geist,
a gust of life. (You get the gist.)

And I like how you let me believe
that you are mine, although it's clear

that you are yours, or even theirs
(whoever that is), and how

your rising and falling accepts
everything (about which we can only

blow gas) that comes your way,
keeping time in my body.

My poem's

feet hurt, especially the right one.
A big corn on its little toe starts
acting up every time it's in any sort of
shoe for more than an hour. Plus,

the big toe knuckle is swollen and angry
from a decade old injury that's turned
arthritic, so that it kills to push. Plus,
the arches on both feet have been falling

for some time, so that by the end of the day
my poem can hardly walk. It just shuffles from
room to room, takes one step at a time up
or down the stairs. It's in way too much pain

to think about anything deep, to bother
saying something about climate collapse or
systemic racism or the cataclysmic separation of
subject from object or the ebbing of democracy,

or to make itself vulnerable by opening up
about some personal issue or loss. No, it just wants
to grab someone, whoever's walking by,
and complain.

Did you ever notice

how, in *The Wizard of Oz*, the bedizened
representatives of the Lollipop Guild never reveal,
nor are even pressed to reveal, their process
of lollipop production? Their art is a wonder,

as is the saturated color of MunchkinLand. Whereas
The Great Oz, a Kansas transplant, offers his American
brand of magic, one based on hoodwink and grift,
one that is surely single-minded and powerful,

but whose secrecy consists of lies, not awe. Thus,
if there really is such a formula, no wonder it must be kept
hush hush, accessible only to initiates. Otherwise
wonder will be made to work the assembly line,

will be bottled up and sold off until it's gone. This is why,
in the "Last Supper" scene in *Don't Look Up*,
the dweeby astrophysicist dad, played by Dicaprio,
can say, right before the comet hits the planet,

splintering into his dining room, "You know,
we really did have everything," and it can still mean
something. It is still a mystery, not a move on
a Hollywood storyboard, not a number

spat out by a logarithm, when and how
and why truth at last reveals itself.

A History Of An Idea

When you are little and the world seems
so full of tall and all-powerful adults,
it makes sense to think of God as one of these
humans, someone much like your parents,

only a little more good and just (and not so
drunk), and a little more beautiful and youthful,
with long hair and a smooth complexion
and a radiantly kind (and not so pissed off) expression.

Then, as you approach and reach adulthood
yourself (how did that ever happen) you find
that this image has also shifted, grown older,
and now wears a long white beard and sits on a throne,

and thus He stays just ahead of you, who are
at any rate running around dropping your kids off
at soccer practices, attending PTA meetings,
making dinner and doing laundry (and drinking

too much and picking fights with your wife),
so that gradually and all of a sudden you are also
very old, and can barely stay on your feet,
and so having caught up to God also sit down

exhausted on your throne in front of the TV
in the so-called living room. This is precisely when
God fools us all and jumps up and runs ahead
and losing His body becomes what He all along

had been, an unimaginable and unknowable
nothing, a mystery, a velvety pocket into which
the universe slipped like a lollipop or pint of whiskey
or tulip bulb or embryo for safekeeping

when He went for a little walk around the block
and out of this world, so you can lose yours.

Where To Send Your Work

When they publish a book on the subject
we can assume the subject is under attack.
When they start a back to nature movement
we can assume that nature's already gone.

Thoreau sits on the threshold of his cabin
and listens to the calls of birds, yes, but mostly
to the whistles of the trains which already
gird him to Concord and Concord to the world.

Davis sits at the kitchen table and waits for
her very short story to arrive. Whitman loafs his soul,
or so he says, although really he's working hard,
squeezing in a few lines while taking care

of his troubled family. Oates lies in a ditch
by a canal. Blake's joys and desires are
being binded by briars. Dickinson, waiting for God
to show up, watches a fly blot out the sun.

Sparrow stands outside the New Yorker
reading his remarkably clear translations
of poems published in the New Yorker,
redefining what it means to make something

public, so that when I finish this poem
all I have to do is open the back door
and read it to the winter garden's birds and mice.
Or you can always leave the city and go

to the outlying districts and, like St. Francis,
hang out with the lepers. Do not fuss over them
or initiate any remedies. Do not act,
but merely and gently kiss their sores.

Looking at

the cardboard coffee cup sleeve
that is supposed to protect me
from the beverage's heat
I never wanted protection from

and don't know how I forgot
to ask at the counter to forgo
in order to save the planet
just a little. It's sitting on this

Starbucks tabletop like
the sloughed off skin of a snake,
or a discarded condom, or a bald tire
in a junkyard, or anything

in a junkyard, or any metaphor
that aims to distract the narrator
and the reader from whatever responsibility
they deem too hot to handle.

Unsafe

You walk out of the classroom,
and when the door closes behind you
(because now all doors, upgraded
to meet safety codes, automatically

close behind you) the leaden thread
between the drone of your teacher
and you is severed cleanly, and you are free
to visit the vending machines or

roam the Senior Hallway or drop in at
the 285 Suite or not, and on your way to nowhere
you see a couple, also severed, entwined
strangely in a recessed doorway,

and at the bottom of the Avenue L stairs
by the Auditorium (because by now you are
very far from the classroom) is a beautifully sour
puddle of cafeteria milk, its carton

stepped on, disfigured, crippled
in the corner, also unsafe and lovely. Your eyes
gratified, you turn to make your way
back to the classroom.

The Unthinking Middle of Everything

Eleven Questions

Does it bother you that dogs pee on the sidewalk?
Do you think that a fallen leaf is dirty?
Do you suspect that contagion lurks on the lips of your lover?
Do you fancy yourself an iconoclast?

Do you sit down on the grass or do you put a blanket down first?
Do you enjoy an occasional slice of chocolate cake?
A pint of ice cream every now and then?
Are you ashamed of what your asshole produces?

Are you ashamed to have an asshole?
Do you secretly think you're an asshole?
What do you produce for the world that does not end up
in a landfill?

I am sorry

I clawed you. Your arms holding me
close to your body seemed so solid and real,

as if they were never going to let me go,
and I was safe. But when I started slipping

away, even while in your embrace, I had to do
something, so I grabbed onto your

forearm and sank my claws in while I helplessly
drifted out of the room. I could see you

down there, inspecting your wound,
carefully disengaging the mirage

of my claw from the mirage of your flesh.
I am somewhat ashamed that drawing

blood from your arm was my last
act on Earth, and wanted to tell you.

Fitful

If you've already made up
your bed and you don't want

to disturb it, don't want those
cool clean smooth sheets

ever rumpled again, eventually,
when it starts to get late and

you're growing tired, you're going
to have to find another place

to lie down and rest, and so
you'll end up sleeping the fitful

sleep of the righteous, every
now and then waking up

on the floor or the couch or
kitchen table or window ledge,

having to remind yourself
that your bed is still tucked in

correctly, still fresh smelling,
so you can fall back asleep.

You can stop

and look at that coffee cup,
the one you are holding in your hand,
the one that is sitting on your desk and imagine the mud
from which it was pinched and shaped
the same way the stories say all of us
were pinched and shaped. Or you can lift it up
and examine, etched into its underside,

the maker's tiny insignia, which,
because it is absolutely incomprehensible
to you, promises something more, something you can't know
or get or own. Or you can notice how its handle,
if that's what it truly is, is in two places crookedly
seamed, where, you imagine, someone,
not you, glued the broken cup back together,

and so can feel all the years and the fragility
and the care inhering in this thing in your hand,
this thing that has weight. This is when the sensation
that whatever it is sitting there within arm's
reach couldn't be farther away from you,
but is exceedingly strange, and may not be
a coffee cup at all, that being a coffee cup

is only its alias, an alibi it uses to get by in this world,
that it was misnamed and put on your shelf,
and you stupidly went along with this blunder
for years, absently sipping from its assumptions
every morning before you went to work. But now
you know, or know you don't know, and can be more
careful and wary, staring at this altogether new

entity in your hand. Or you can go on looking at
the cup as cup, as ordinary coffee cup, and use it as you will,
and when you get bored with it, you can put it out
on the stoop and buy a new one. For this is the order
of the ordinary. Everything lines up to be used and discarded,
used and discarded, and that is all. And that is
not strange at all.

Dear Randy,

Thank you for showing me there's nothing to save.
This frees up a lot of time on Sunday mornings
and pulls that abscessed molar out by its bloody roots,
for if I'm already submerged in the ocean,

if all manner of sea creatures are already flitting
and darting by me on the corner of M and East 17th,
if what I was holding onto is already salted and leeched,
and what's left of that bleached and weightless,

and will last forever, lightly tumbling along the sandy floor
with every gently undulant and enormously inertial
tug of that body,
then why this dread of drowning?

Purr

The way the cat houdinis
her way out of the straightjacket of

your embrace and stalks off
and turns and glares at you,

and then circles back and starts
headbutting your hand,

which, because you're accustomed to
these shenanigans, is prepared

to apply the right amount
and kind of contact, the amount

and kind the cat has determined,
which is to say, gently with

your bent forefinger between
her ears, makes you wonder

if the ups and downs of your
emotional life aren't also a game

you've been trained to enjoy,
and there's nothing wrong.

Deno's Wonder Hole

I dug a hole
and put all of humanity,

which includes you,
in it. If you

want to get out you
can show this stub

of a poem to me
as proof. I will be

the one standing by the gate,
dressed in blue jeans

and Metallica T-shirt,
bored out of my mind,

waiting for you to shriek
or beg for release,

or for whatever
is in your pockets

to spill and clatter
on the cement.

The way the pillows on the couch

first thing in the morning lying there disarranged
specifically by the previous night's events
greet you and ask you to behold them
before you put them back where they supposedly go.
The way you answer that greeting is political.

The way you write in your notebook,
whether you plan what it is you're going to say
or just put down the next word that comes to you,
is also political. Making things line up
can be political. The things that stick and collect

about the drain of the sink, speckling the white
ceramic tiling is political. Of course the kind of cereal
you eat is political. An egg with all its heft
and potentiality hidden in your palm
is also political, as is the rooster's cry. Or

maybe you prefer the phone in the morning,
so that you can choose your own ringtone: stargaze,
slowrise, summit, twinkle, uplift, aurora, bamboo,
circles, churches, input, keys, popcorn, pulse, alert,
classic, bell, bloom, calypso, chime, choo choo,

descent, dog, electronic, fanfare, glass, horn,
ladder, minuet, newsflash, noir, survival, spell,
forest, suspense, swish, swoosh, telegraph,
tip toes, twisted, typewriter, updates, are also political,
but in a particularly fruitless and artificial way.

The choices we make are political
although to choose from a menu is always to eat
what they want you to eat. They never want you to eat
the peanut butter and jelly sandwich,
which you can make yourself at home.

To be guided

you have to look for the little guidances
buried in the day: how the dog lunges

enormously after the small, in your eyes,
event of a squirrel; how the birds are making

such a gregarious racket, congregating
in the bare, late winter shrubbery on this

sparkling February day; how the mud is
plastic and receives the imprint of the sole

of your shoe just so, so that thus you unwittingly
participate in this guidance, leaving a trail

of letters, which, linked, spell words for
those who follow you to puzzle over. For the new

assumption is that for you to live and have
a voice in the world, the world must also

live and have a voice which you yourself
must listen to. Look, even now,

little green guidances are shyly
pushing their tips out of the earth.

The War at Home

The tips of bayonets gleam
in the doorway. I pause my instruction,

walk to the back of the classroom,
and tell the pink-cheeked camo-clad idiots

that we're trying to carry on our class discussion,
that if they'd like to come in and sit down

and join in they're welcome, but that otherwise
they need to carry out their negative fantasies

somewhere else, etc. They stare at me
through those weird night goggles

characters in first person shooting games wear,
so I wave them away and close the door

and return to our question: "Does the sky
inspire us precisely because it is an optical illusion,

its powder blue giving a dimension and limit
to the infinite, a kind of roof that makes the world

a chapel and us its purposeful worshippers,
or because it is so menacingly and astoundingly

empty it demands our obeisance?" Before any
of the students can respond a hand grenade

flies through the window and bounces on the floor,
toddling to a stop by my feet. I pick it up

and walk to the window and throw it back out
and shout, "I don't mind it if you boys want to engage

in recreation. Indeed, I believe that the art
of happiness is tripartite, consisting of physical,

mental and spiritual practices, and that all
three are equally crucial. Therefore, by all means,

play on, but please restrict your grenade play
to your grenade play area." The device

detonating in the street below, I was unable
to hear their response. Yet, to my delight,

while I was engaged in this interaction,
table one, the Ineffables, had been preparing

an answer: "But Mr. Elliot, if the self
is a mere hallucination being projected

on the screen at the back of the mind
of every individual, and if this entertainment

is kept going only as long as the individual
can stay in motion, doing this and doing that,

worrying about this and worrying about that,
then wouldn't this very kind of class discussion,

that wants to step back and see everything all at once,
necessarily invite the self-liquidation of each

of its participants, youthful students sitting here
at desks in good faith?" It was at this exact moment

that the Putin Tank burst through the wall, scattering
youth, and turned its turret, its barrel taking aim

at the notes on the board, which had been organized
into an impromptu radiating map of words and arrows

and underlined double question marks and fragile
stick figures meant to indicate some important idea

or other, the kind of thing one routinely erases
when the bell rings. Nevertheless, the mute vehicle

did not wait for the bell, but suddenly spoke its flaming,
deafening word, which the classroom easily heard

and obeyed, opening a hole in the wall through which
this communication could presumably continue.

Paradise

My rib keeps me awake.
It keeps saying it wants to be my handmaiden.
But I don't want a handmaiden.
I don't need a handmaiden.
What I need is some sleep
so I can get up and work tomorrow.

So because I am up I hold the screen door
to the backyard open, and although there are only
three days until Spring and it's 60 out
and the birds have started their chanting
in the early morning darkness,
the cat is crazy and keeps circling and circling
on the threshold, as if what he had wanted all along
wasn't to actually go
outside, but for me to stand there
holding the door, doing his bidding.

There is so much for me in this mutual aid
paradise. I can always scoop the litter
or change a light bulb
or separate the stuff on the table into piles
or push in chairs or fold and put away
the towels that having been drying overnight
on the hallway railing. It is thus I spend my days in love
with my life,
with the dark mystery of morning,
with the sharp ache in my side.

The two halves of my rib are crying out for each for other,
which is a sound I feel every time I move a muscle,
a muscle I hadn't known was there,
a muscle that was contentedly doing its job,
hardly noticed, unacknowledged. There is no God,
only a loose confederation of muscle and molecule.
There are no Lords or Ladies,
only these self-employed Ladies-in-waiting,
these stubbornly undividable handmaidens like me,
each living within the circle of her own horizon,
each baking a tray or two of cookies
to bring to the sale at school.

For the hen

the overwhelming urge is to hurry back
to the coop and sit on the egg
and brood, so that the trouble grows,
takes on characteristics, hatches.

But what then? You'll end up feeding
and tending the chick until it is big
and plump and ready for slaughter. No,
resist the urge. Lift yourself up

off the egg. Walk away. Gather all
your courage and strength and let
it sit there, alone, in the silent, dim shack
at the back of the yard, a little light

coming in through the crack between
the warped old boards. Deprived
of the warmth of your interaction, this
nothing will become nothing.

George is trying to get

a rise out of Clara. Ranger
is yowling from the top
of the stairs. Anne is up,
padding to the bathroom,

and therefore Snoopy is
about to start in on his
earnest barking for breakfast.
This also means Greta

will soon be following Anne
down the stairs and start
herding and competing
with Snoopy for attention

and food and love. Walter
is on the can, door open,
taking care of business,
which can take quite a while

since listening to highlights
from last night's Celtics
game is an essential part of
his ritual. Then there's me, worrying

about whether, with all these
bodies, I should make more
coffee, and how I'm going to
write a poem now.

Waking Up

At first we thought, because he'd wander
about the house, crying pointlessly, bumping into
legs, getting extraordinarily underfoot, nudging up
stupidly and dangerously close to the dogs
when they were eating, that he was going blind.
We'd go to him and pick him up and his eyes
would be wild and unfocused. We'd pass our hands
across his line of vision. Nothing. Then he started
to lose weight and get bony and stiff and stopped
taking good care of himself, his long marmalade hair
getting all dreaded up and his cute white boots
filthy, and we thought maybe he was sick. So we
brought him in, and the vet said, No, Ranger's in
excellent health, especially for a 20 year old cat,
and he's not blind. What he's got is CIS, Cognitive
Impairment Syndrome, an early phase of dementia.
He suggested we start feeding him wet food to fight
the weight loss and brush his hair more often and
to manually undo the knots and even showed us
how to carefully snip the more stubborn ones to assist
in his grooming. This made sense, explaining his
wide-eyed look and his recurring high volume
bouts of panic. Maybe he's disoriented, we thought.
Maybe he keeps forgetting who he is and where he is.
Maybe this is why he sits at the top of the stairs
and starts yowling inconsolably into the dark
echo chamber of the stairwell at 3:00 in the morning.
Maybe this is why, even though Anne wakes up
and starts calling Ranger! Ranger! Ranger! Ranger!
from our bed and then George wakes up and tells

Anne to shut up from the warmth of his room,
Ranger keeps on yowling and yowling, as if
he's involved in some life and death struggle.
Maybe this explains how, when I get out of bed
and walk down the hall to pick him up from his pulpit
and hold him close, and holding him close
is the only thing that works, the only thing that
calms him and eases his desperation, so that
he starts purring quietly and his eyes narrow
into contented slits. Maybe my smell and touch
are things he still remembers, things that can
reorient him, and tell him who he is. Or maybe,
I think, feeling his weightless and fragile frame
in my arms, and wondering how something so
insubstantial can produce such a terrific alarm,
the very old know something we don't know,
something they wake up and see in the middle of the night,
something they need to tell us.

Thus Lost

When I go to the park
and sit on the bench by the lake
and close my eyes, I start to hear
the sounds of birds,

start to distinguish the abrupt
rusty crrrrk of the starling from
the gently sharp chpchpcheeps
of the industrious sparrow from

the conspiratorial caw of the crow
from the singsongy feebee of
the roosted chickadee from the
lonely wails of gulls circling overhead,

miles from the sea, and from all
the others I'm not identifying now,
an unknown area that implies
an infinite largesse, a continuous

thicket, of birds and their calls
throughout the park, the city, the continent, all
populating this moment's Earth, all
calling out whether or not I get to be

the one paying attention. But when
I open my eyes and everything rushes
in and I start to think of what I have
to do today, what I should have

said to that person when that person
said what he said to me, all that
bird song seems to have disappeared,
although, of course, it hasn't.

Even when I've made my way home,
and am well indoors, sitting before
my computer screen, trying to solve
the same compulsive problem

I solved the day before, even when
I'm thus lost, I can close my eyes
and know the world is busy with birds
and filled with their song.

Proudhon

It's an act of theft
to record the way the morning

sun splashes the table,
the way the few dead leaves

still clinging to a branch
quiver in the breeze,

the achingly unknowable way
some bird is crying to some

other bird, the way the cabin
nestles among the scrub pine and oak,

when the sun, the leaf, and the bird
have not signed a waiver.

The cabin, however, nestling
among these scrub pine and oak,

is merely a piece of property
disguised as an authentic cabin

nestled among the scrub pine
and oak, and therefore should not be

confused with a nest, or even a home,
and thus may be described freely,

without fear of penalty, obligation,
or any observance of rights.

Such as it is,

bounded at either end
by nothingness,

by two enormous
invisibly black hands

warmly and lovingly
holding me and making me

stay put for a while.
So I don't panic

and fly off somewhere,
they let me every

now and then think
I can feel them.

Otherwise

Otherwise you're buying
a house in Levittown,

which isn't really a choice,
the market forces and your fear

of the old neighborhood
(a healthy fear, really),

and your determination
to never go backwards,

(which is positive and admirable and
American), drove you there.

You got out of the car,
which was also new,

a '48 Chrysler, and breathed
in the air of authenticity.

But what the lot really
needed was some trees,

and a pollinator garden,
and a river that bends

and deepens into a pool
where you might take a dip,

dip yourself entirely and
make yourself new.

Otherwise a time machine
so you could travel back

and keep your parents
from meeting and having kids.

What I Am Doing

When the Universe cried, "I'm so lonely!
Isn't there anyone out there for me?"
she was met with a dense silence
that was entirely appropriate.

For who would want to conjugate
irregular verbs all afternoon
with Sister Mary Theresa,
stern in that spritely way

though she may be? So when she added, "Who?
Who will be my lover?" Everyone else,
in order to preserve their particular
identities, their identifiable

particularities, where brushing one's teeth
is brushing one's teeth and driving
to work is driving to work, took
one step back, leaving me

all alone with her. And here I am,
forty-eight years later, and
what I'm doing is never
what I'm doing.

for D. Nurkse

When a non-poet dies,
you're left with their furniture,

their rugs, paintings, pots and pans,
shirt and shoes, coats, photos,

and a few stories strangers
tell about them at a ceremony

you're never ready for, all
of which, of course, is nothing,

for you don't have them.
But when a poet reaches the end,

you're left with their poems,
as well, which can keep you

close to them, sometimes
bring you even closer

than you were to them
when they were alive.

You take off your coat and tie
and start to go through a poem,

and that is when their deepest
and best part comes rushing back

to you, and you feel you finally
understand them, and maybe

even yourself. It's as if they weren't really
here when they were here,

and now that they're gone,
they're really really here.

Boric acid

works great! You just sprinkle
the powder in a high activity

area and wait. Soon enough, one of them
will scamper through the fine dust,

which, electromagnetized, will cling to
their feet and limbs, their exoskeleton,

which they'll then have to start cleaning.
Thus the dust enters and quickly

erodes their nervous system, melts their
innards, and they perish. The others,

emerging from their nest
to scrupulously ingest

their fallen brethren, soon follow suit.
This point of view is why Codrescu

suggests that if we write, we write
as if we were already dead.

Butterflies In Your Stomach

The constant precariousness of utterance,
the overwhelming tendency towards silence,
the ever shifting space between being
and not being, makes even the perfectly
commonplace phrase, even the bald cliche,
because it's always on the verge of extinction,
take on new and urgent significance.

This is why we need war,
why we need every now and then to perform an emergency
Caesarian deep in the forest, slicing open
the burgeoning teenage poet's belly to release
a kaleidoscope of pollinators back into
the world, and why we have to go on fluttering
in the unthinking middle of everything.

Personna

becoming a person implies
finding a way to project your voice
so you can be heard

implies covering your face
and putting on a character
so you can be recognized and read

implies an audience you're playing to
the other half of an interaction
real or imagined

implies an implacable story
in which you're only playing your part
saying your lines

implies an original sorting process
the mother and son walking into a dim barn
where the props are kept

she points to the good one
he puts it on and looks at her
she shakes her head no

and points to the bad one
which he again tries on
and again she shakes her head

and points to the lost one
which he puts on easily and she smiles
yes and leaves him

for Douglas

People use their phones now
as if they're talking to themselves,

not to you, who ends up
alone in a room, listening

to the voice of the other go
on and on. This is the conundrum

of the ghost. You notice everyone else,
but nobody notices you. You

are disappointed Hansel and Gretel
fail to be eaten. It's not fair

they get to push the witch into the oven
in the end when they are so clearly

in the wrong. What are they doing,
wandering around in the woods? Why

are they using breadcrumbs, of all things,
to mark their way? What are they

thinking? They should be the ones served
for dinner. Instead, the old woman

ends up roasted. Why can they have their cake
and eat it? Do they really need to carry

assault rifles into abortion clinics
and shoot up patients and doctors?

Shouldn't they be required to bring
the fetuses home and raise them

as their own, fattening them up
in front of their wide wide screens?

In Memory of Your Birthdays
for Josie, 4/1/55–11/14/19

When we used to put an egg in your shoe,
aluminum foil everything in your office,
affix a life-size Burt Reynolds in his famous odalisque pose
on your bedroom wall,

when the mug we'd serve your morning tea in would insist on dribbling,
when we'd take out the cream from each Oreo
and replace it with toothpaste and pack the new cookies
back up and leave the box on the counter and wait,

when we'd short-sheet your bed,
put food coloring in your shower head,
move your green Toyota in the middle of the night to the patio by the pool
and put gigantic cardboard sunglasses on its windshield,

when we'd secure a little packet of salt
under the lid of the pepper shaker
and a little packet of pepper
under the lid of the salt shaker,

when we'd loosen the tops of all the condiments in the fridge,
when we'd change the time on all the clocks
and get up at 3:00 am and make a lot of noise,
pretending it was 8:00 am and time to go to Church,

when a letter from the President of the United States would arrive
for you in the mail asking for your advice on a personal matter,
when we'd replace the front page of the Times Union with a facsimile
announcing the arrival of Aliens from Saturn and the need for
   immediate evacuation,

when we'd bake a beautiful cake and affix
a single candle on top, for it was always April 1st,
and you'd blow that lone candle out,
and it would light itself again.

JOE ELLIOT teaches English and lives in Brooklyn with hs wife, Anne Noonan, and their two dogs, Greta and Snoopy. He is the author of numerous chapbooks, including: *You Gotta Go In It's the Big Game, Poems to be Centered on Much Much Larger Pieces of Paper, 15 Clanking Radiators, 14 Knots, Reduced, Half Gross* (a collaboration with artist John Koos), and *Object Lesson* (a collaboration with artist Rich O'Russa). Granary Books published *If It Rained Here* (a collaboration with artist Julie Harrison). His long poem, *101 Designs for the World Trade Center*, was published by Faux Press as an e-book in 2003. Collections of his work include *Opposable Thumb* (subpress, 2006), *Homework* (Lunar Chandelier, 2010), and *Idea for a B Movie* (Free Scholars Press, 2016).

www.ingramcontent.com/pod-product-compliance
Lightning Source LLC
Chambersburg PA
CBHW031218120626
46545CB00003B/903